It's chaos!

Elspeth Graham

OXFORD
UNIVERSITY PRESS

OXFORD
UNIVERSITY PRESS

is a department of the University of Oxford.
It furthers the University's objective of excellence in research, scholarship,
and education by publishing worldwide in

Oxford   New York
Auckland   Cape Town   Dar es Salaam   Hong Kong   Karachi
Kuala Lumpur   Madrid   Melbourne   Mexico City   Nairobi
New Delhi   Shanghai   Taipei   Toronto

With offices in

Argentina   Austria   Brazil   Chile   Czech Republic   France   Greece
Guatemala   Hungary   Italy   Japan   Poland   Portugal   Singapore
South Korea   Switzerland   Thailand   Turkey   Ukraine   Vietnam

Acknowledgements

The publisher would like to thank the following for permission to reproduce photographs: **p3** Friedrich Saurer/Science Photo Library; **p4** (c)Museum of Fine Arts, Boston, Massachusetts, USA/William Sturgis Bigelow Collection/Bridgeman Art Library; **p4/5**bgrnd NASA Marshall Space Flight Center (NASA-MSFC)/ NASA; **p5**t Visual Arts Library (London)/Alamy, **p5**b Reto Stockli/Alan Nelson/Fritz Hasler./NASA; **p6** Science Museum/AKG - Images; **p7** Peter Dazeley/The Image Bank/Getty Images; **p7**bgrnd Christoph Weiser/Alamy; **p8**l Godfrey Argent Studio/Royal Society, **p8**r /AKG – Images ; **p9** Bettmann/Corbis UK Ltd.; **p10/11**bgrnd Friedrich Saurer/Science Photo Library; **p11**t Gregory Sams/Science Photo Library, **p11**b Alfred Pasieka/Science Photo Library; **p12**l ImageState/Alamy, **p12**r Cheryl Lorenz; **p12/13**bgrnd Bill Bachman/Alamy; **p14/15**bgrnd Alfred Pasieka/Science Photo Library; **p17**t Trevor Smithers ARPS/ Alamy, **p17**b isifa Image Service s.r.o./Alamy; **p19**t James Osmond/Alamy, **p19**c Carr Clifton/Minden Pictures/Frank Lane Picture Agency; **p19**b Jim Brandenburg/Minden Pictures/Frank Lane Picture Agency; **p20**tl&tr&b Kenneth Libbrecht/Science Photo Library; **p20/21**bgrnd Jamie Farrant/iStockphoto; **p21** Tom Morrison/Stone/Getty Images; **p22**bl Kenneth Libbrecht/Science Photo Library, **p22**br&t Kenneth Libbrecht/Science Photo Library; **p22/23** Tim Pannell/Corbis UK Ltd.; **p23**tl&tr&cr&b Kenneth Libbrecht/ Science Photo Library; **p24**bgrnd Alfred Pasieka/Science Photo Library

Cover: Alamy/tompiodesign.com

Illustrations by Bill Bolton/Advocate: **p6, p13, p14, p18**; Peter Bull Art Studio: **p10, p15, p16**

Contents

In the beginning there was chaos

Many myths and legends tell of the world's **creation**. Often, these stories begin with a wild, dark **chaos**. Out of this chaos light and shape emerge and form a world we can live in.

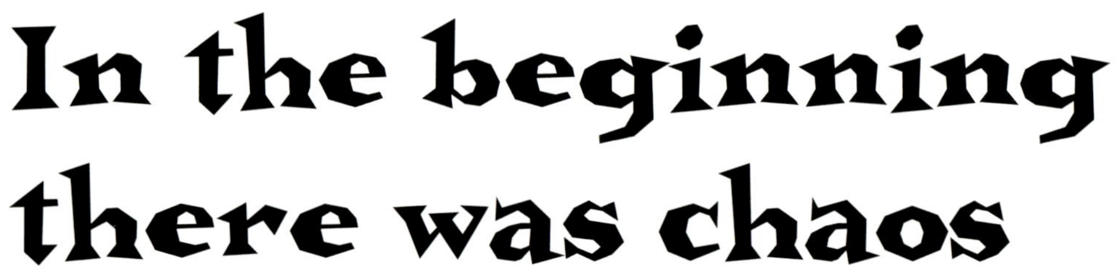

The Japanese believed that the gods Izagani and Izanami created order from chaos.

A state of disorder

Order has always been thought of as good and disorder (chaos) as bad. In many **cultures** there is an **eternal** battle between the two opposites: good and evil.

If you had to choose to live in a world ruled by either order or chaos, which would you choose?

Under the Wave off Kanagawa by Katsushika Hokusai shows the chaos of a stormy sea.

Throughout history people have explored the world and tried to make sense of it. They looked for order in their lives and in the world they lived in. We all still do this and probably always will.

To bring order out of chaos, scientists and mathematicians looked for the natural rules and laws that make our world tick.

Is the world made of clockwork?

Three hundred and fifty years ago the great scientist Sir Isaac Newton (1642–1727) sat by an apple tree and watched an apple fall. He wondered why it fell and realised that it was because it was attracted to the Earth. There was a force, called gravity, that pulled down the apple – and this force affects everything else on Earth.

Newton's law of gravity is a simple but very important idea. Newton had found order in chaos. He then wanted to discover the system that made the whole world work. He wanted to discover 'The Theory of Everything'.

Newton's discoveries led most of the scientists who lived and worked after him to imagine that the world was like a gigantic clockwork machine.

These were exciting times for scientists as more and more was understood about how our world works. The laws of sound, light, **magnetism** and electricity were discovered and tested. Scientific knowledge was growing fast.

Calculations and more calculations

By the 1920s, scientists and mathematicians had worked out many of the rules of the natural world. To use these rules, and be able to **predict** how the world would behave, scientists had to make billions and billions of calculations.

In 1922 Lewis Richardson, an English scientist, tried to use mathematical rules to predict the weather. He imagined a weather factory where an army of people worked non-stop using desk calculators to make their calculations. He estimated that it would take 64,000 people to predict the weather at the same speed at which the weather actually happened!

Adding machine, 1914

Computers were what people were waiting for – with computers, scientists and mathematicians could do billions of calculations very fast.

Large, slow computer, 1955

Computers can now calculate in megaflops – a megaflop is one million calculations per second. Some computers run at 800 megaflops – imagine how long it would take to work out that number of calculations without a computer!

Side by side

However, early scientists had been mistaken!

The invention and use of computers showed that the world was very different to the one they'd imagined – it was far more interesting than a clockwork world. Instead of the neat order that they'd expected to find, scientists were amazed and delighted (some of them were confused and a bit cross) to see the strange and mysterious patterns of chaos, dancing across their computer screens.

Chaos had always been there but no one had looked for it. When scientists began to use computers they often found very **unpredictable** behaviour where they had expected to find order.

Stranger still was that this chaotic behaviour was also filled with patterns – patterns that were familiar and new, but rich and strange – all at the same time.

Chaos can be found everywhere in nature, but there is order too. The world is not ruled by order, nor is it ruled by chaos. Order and chaos exist side by side.

It was a **meteorologist**, a weather forecaster, who first glimpsed chaos and recognized it for what it was.

The meteorologist

Edward Lorenz was an American mathematician, who was fascinated by everything to do with the weather.

The weather affects every living thing on the planet. By the 1960s scientists knew how the weather worked; they knew how clouds were formed, what made it rain, how storms happened. But what they didn't know was what the weather would do next. They could make guesses – but they were often wrong.

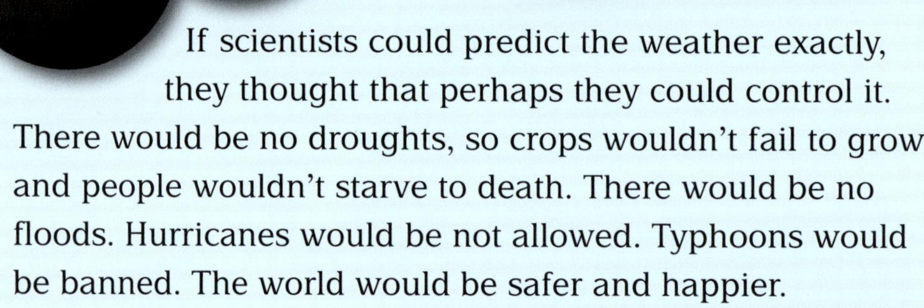

If scientists could predict the weather exactly, they thought that perhaps they could control it. There would be no droughts, so crops wouldn't fail to grow and people wouldn't starve to death. There would be no floods. Hurricanes would be not allowed. Typhoons would be banned. The world would be safer and happier.

Would the world be safer? Maybe things would get **sinister**…

Meteorologists, too, were excited by the possibilities that computers promised.

Like many great discoveries, chaos was discovered by accident. Edward Lorenz was trying to discover the secrets of long term weather predictions. He believed that if data about all the present weather conditions were fed into a computer, then future patterns could be predicted accurately.

A storm in a coffee cup

In the 1960s, Edward Lorenz used one of the very first computers to create his own weather system. He programmed the computer to invent imaginary weather patterns. He fed into the computer twelve weather rules (mathematical **equations**) to do with features like wind speed, temperature and air pressure. Then he watched the weather patterns develop and change.

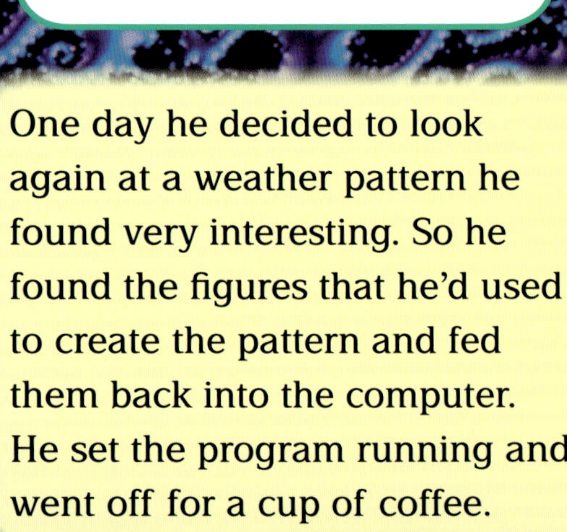

One day he decided to look again at a weather pattern he found very interesting. So he found the figures that he'd used to create the pattern and fed them back into the computer. He set the program running and went off for a cup of coffee.

When he came back he found chaos! He was
startled to see that the second weather pattern
was completely, crazily, different from the first
one. He'd expected them to be exactly the same!

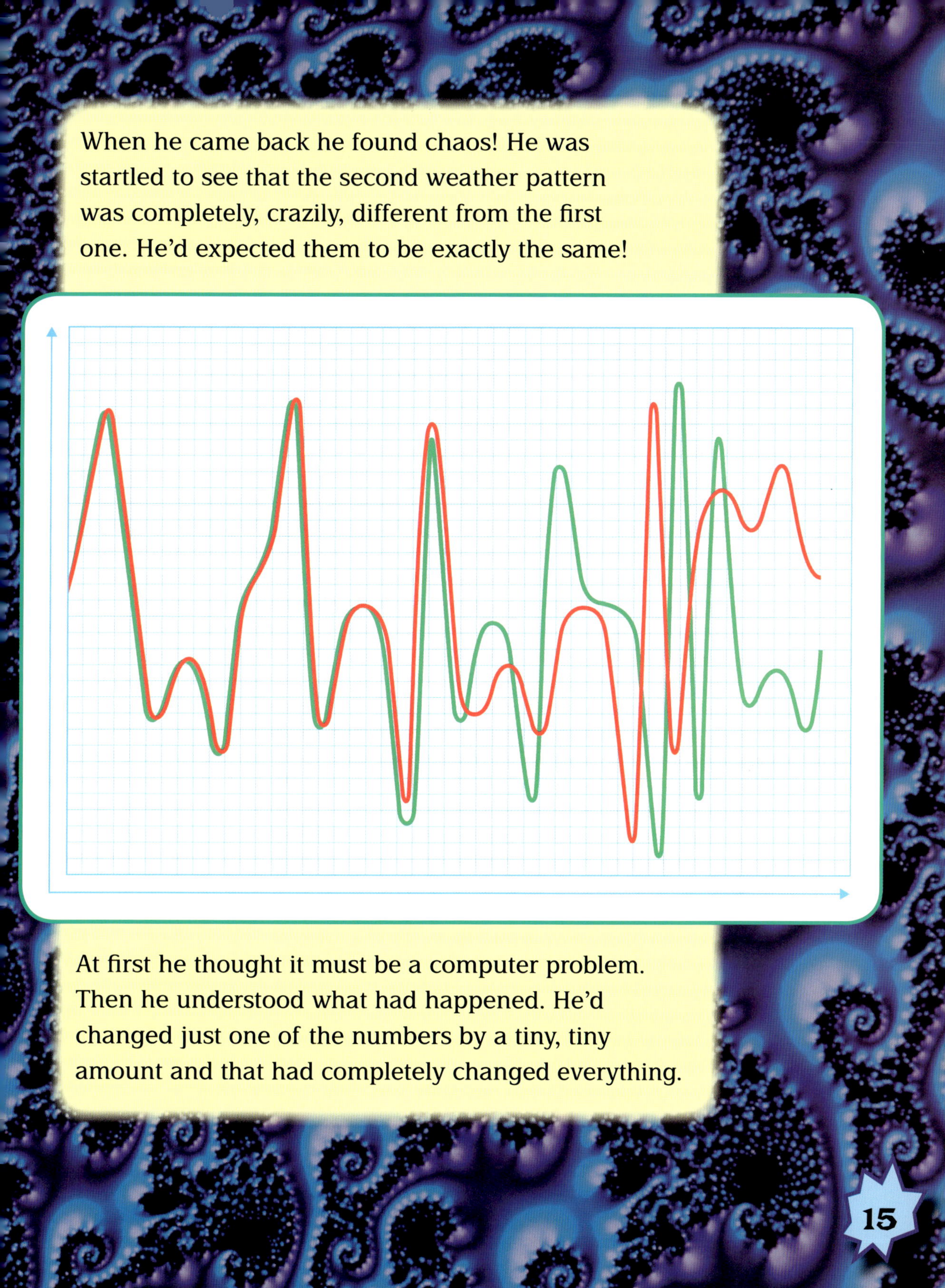

At first he thought it must be a computer problem.
Then he understood what had happened. He'd
changed just one of the numbers by a tiny, tiny
amount and that had completely changed everything.

The butterfly effect

What Edward Lorenz realised was that long term weather predicting is not possible. It's only possible to predict the weather for a few days ahead. That's because a very, very small event can cause huge changes to the patterns of the world's weather.

This small event might be no more than a tiny puff of wind or even the movement of air caused by a butterfly flapping its wings. If, for example, a butterfly in Mexico could cause rain in Texas by changing the **initial conditions** of the weather, then the weather can't be predictable.

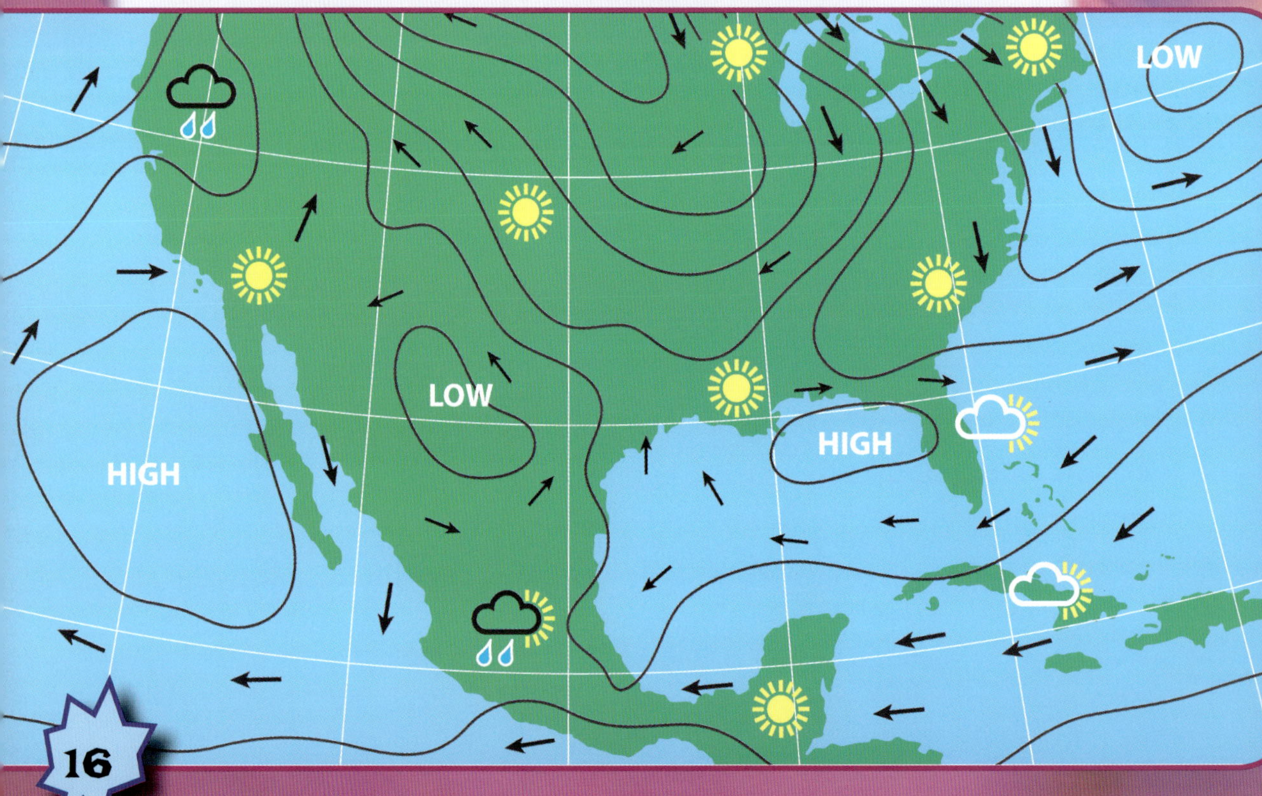

Lorenz's discovery became known as the Butterfly Effect. Scientists now call it 'sensitive dependence on initial conditions'.

Long ago, an unknown poet put it this way:

For want of a nail, the shoe was lost;
For want of a shoe, the horse was lost;
For want of a horse, the rider was lost;
For want of a rider, the battle was lost;
For want of a battle, the kingdom was lost!

Pooh sticks

An easy way to understand the importance of
initial conditions is by playing 'Pooh sticks'.
The rules for playing 'Pooh sticks' are very simple:
❋ Any number of people can play.
❋ Find sticks that are the same sort of size.
❋ Count to three and drop the sticks from a bridge
   into a stream or a river at the same time.

The sticks will start to fall down into the water together, but then they will have very different journeys. The sticks tumble and twist as they fall. Gusts of wind push and tug at them. They splash into the stream in different places and at different moments and at different angles.

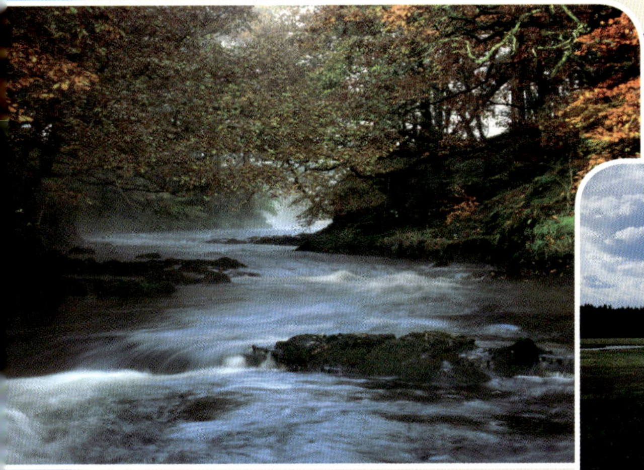

The stream can be fast-flowing...

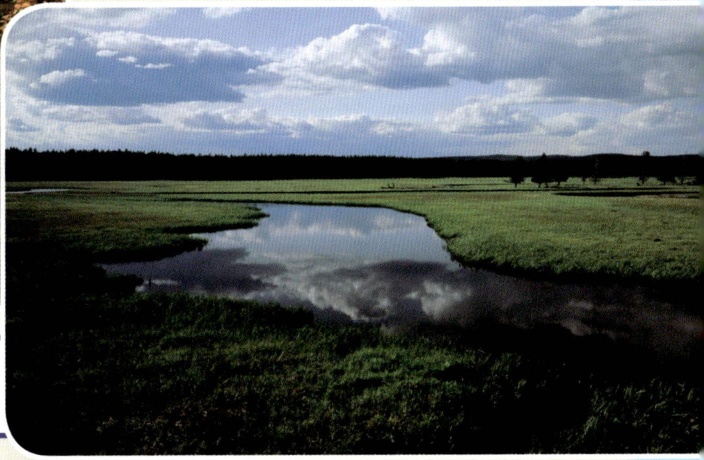

...or slow-moving.

The way the water moves along is very complicated. It swirls and coils, and flows slightly faster in one place than in another. Stones beneath the water create ripples and bubbles. One stick may drift swiftly under the bridge and be the winner. The other may be caught in a swirl and left behind in a still pool of water beside the bank.

Turbulence can make the water swirl about.

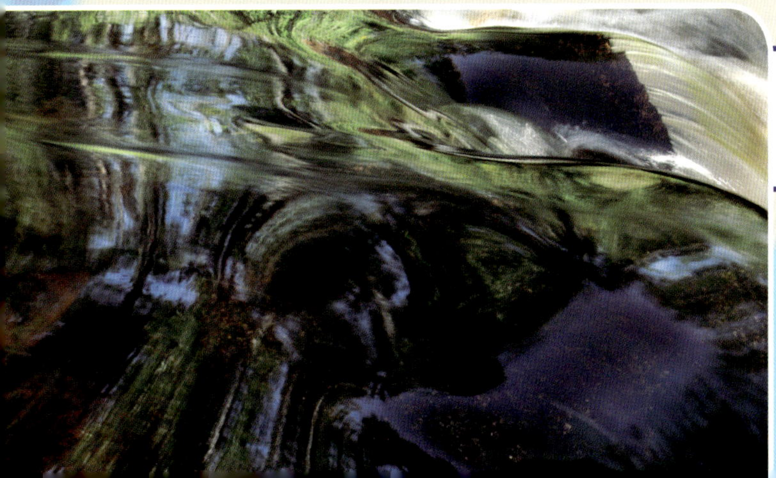

Snowflakes

Snowflakes
are all different.
No two are
ever exactly
the same.

But *why* are no two snowflakes identical? It's because of the importance of initial conditions.

As a growing snowflake falls to Earth it floats in the wind and is whisked to and fro for an hour or longer. It is whirled about by air turbulence, by gusts of wind, and each snowflake takes a different path down to the ground. The speed of its fall will change, moment by moment. It may even be lifted upwards for a second or two.

20

The snowflake will pass through patches of air that are wetter than others. It will bump into tiny particles left in the air by dust or smoke or pollution. All these things will make a difference to the way the snowflake grows. They are all tiny events on the snowflake's journey.

When at last it settles on the ground, its final shape is the record of this journey through the winter sky. Because no two journeys are exactly the same, no two snowflakes are exactly the same. Each one is **unique**. Snowflakes are born in chaos and formed by chaos.

Beautiful chaos

Lorenz knew he had discovered something enormously important. He wrote an article about his discovery and it was published. But it was published in a meteorology magazine and there it remained not read or not understood for a long time.

Lorenz was ahead of his time. He 'opened a door' that showed us a new world, and for years no one looked through it.

When more and more people started to have computers, chaos became impossible to miss. Chaos theory, 'the amazing science of the unpredictable,' emerged as a new science in the 1970s. Chaos had been seen and recognised.

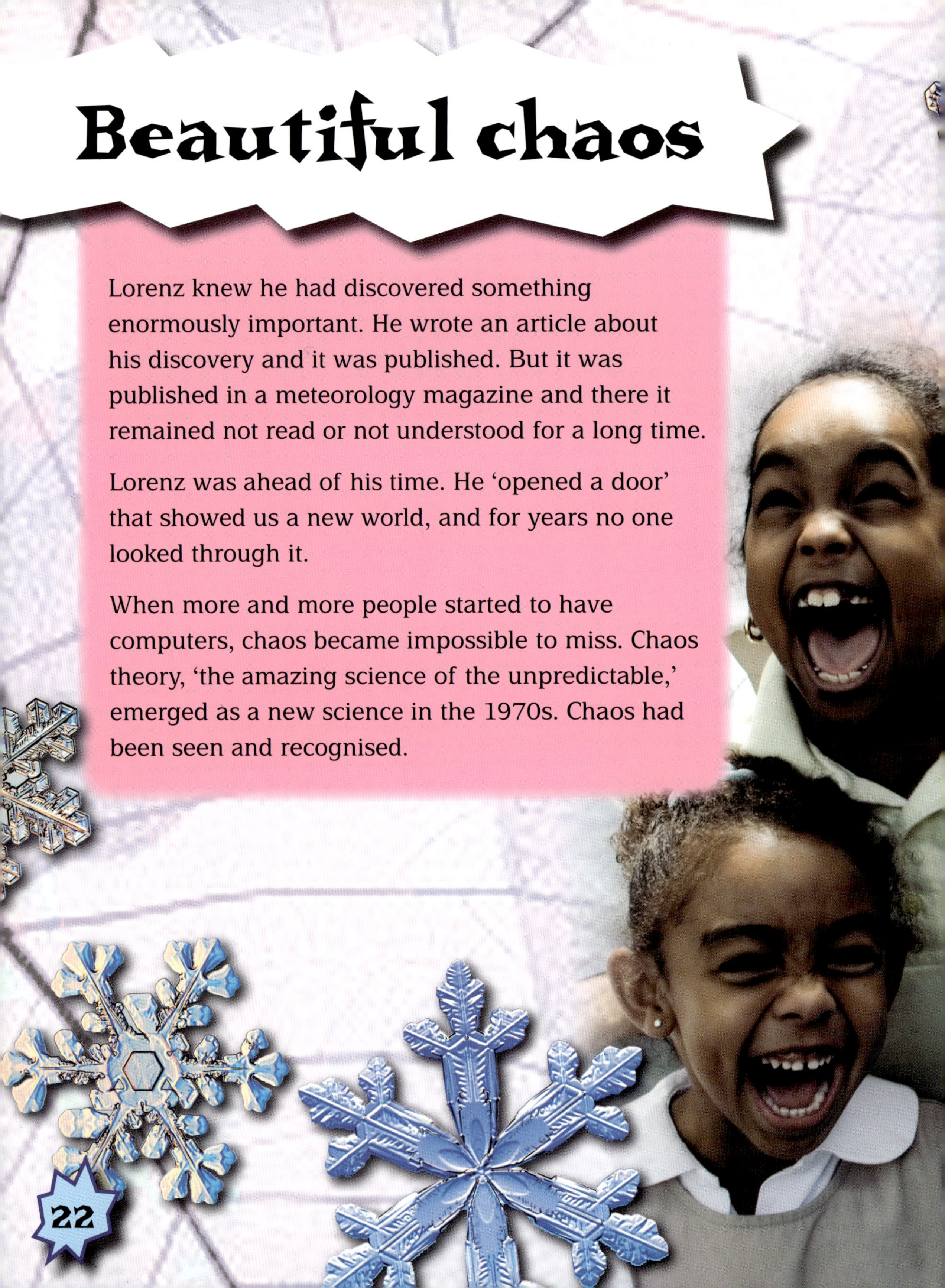

Chaos is as important to our world as order. We and the world we live in are formed by chaos, just like snowflakes.

23

Glossary

chaos – a state of disorder
creation – the beginning of the world and all living things
cultures – different groups of people
equations – mathematical sentences which show that two statements are equal
eternal – going on forever
initial conditions – the state something is in at its beginning
magnetism – the force of attraction between a magnet and an object
meteorologist – a scientist who studies the weather
predict – to guess or forecast in advance
sinister – threatening danger or evil
turbulence – constant movement and flow, unsettled
unique – the only one of its kind
unpredictable – difficult or impossible to predict or forecast

Index